COURAGEOUS CHILDREN AND WOMEN OF THE AMERICAN REVOLUTION— THROUGH PRIMARY SOURCES

John Micklos, Jr.

 Enslow Publishers, Inc.
40 Industrial Road
Box 398
Berkeley Heights, NJ 07922
USA
http://www.enslow.com

Original edition published as *The Brave Women and Children of the American Revolution* in 2009.

Library of Congress Cataloging-in-Publication Data

Micklos, John.
  Courageous children and women of the American Revolution : through primary sources / John Micklos, Jr.
      p. cm. — (The American Revolution through primary sources)
  Summary: "Discusses the lives and roles of children and women during the American Revolution, including life and work on the home front, women nurses and soldiers, and children spying and fighting in the war" —Provided by publisher.
  "Original edition published as The brave women and children of the American Revolution in 2008"—T.p. verso.
   Includes bibliographical references and index.
  ISBN 978-0-7660-4131-8
  1. United States—History—Revolution, 1775–1783—Participation, Female—Juvenile literature. 2. United States—History—Revolution, 1775–1783—Women—Juvenile literature. 3. United States—History—Revolution, 1775–1783—Participation, Juvenile—Juvenile literature. 4. United States—History—Revolution, 1775–1783—Children—Juvenile literature. 5. Women—United States—History—18th century—Juvenile literature. 6. Children—United States—History—18th century—Juvenile literature. 7. Spies—United States—History—18th century—Juvenile literature. I. Micklos, John. Brave women and children of the American Revolution. II. Title.
  E276.M53 2013
  973.3083—dc23

                              2012022379

Future editions:
Paperback ISBN 978-1-4644-0189-3
ePUB ISBN 978-1-4645-1102-8
PDF ISBN 978-1-4646-1102-5

Printed in the United States of America.

082012 Lake Book Manufacturing, Inc., Melrose Park, IL

10 9 8 7 6 5 4 3 2 1

To Our Readers: We have done our best to make sure all Internet Addresses in this book were active and appropriate when we went to press. However, the author and the publisher have no control over and assume no liability for the material available on those Internet sites or on other Web sites they may link to. Any comments or suggestions can be sent by email to comments@enslow.com or to the address on the back cover.

♻ Enslow Publishers, Inc., is committed to printing our books on recycled paper. The paper in every book contains 10% to 30% post-consumer waste (PCW). The cover board on the outside of each book contains 100% PCW. Our goal is to do our part to help young people and the environment too!

Illustration Credits: Clements Library, University of Michigan, p. 39; Clipart.com, a division of Getty Images, p. 32; Domenick D'Andrea, courtesy of the National Guard, pp. 3, 13, 28; The Granger Collection, NYC, pp. 23, 33; Courtesy of Hargrett Rare Book and Manuscript Library / University of Georgia Libraries, p. 38; Library of Congress Prints and Photographs, pp. 1, 4, 5, 14, 19, 21, 25, 31, 35; Morton Fox, p. 36; Courtesy National Park Service, Adams National Historic Park, p. 9; Courtesy National Park Service, Museum Management Program and Guilford Courthouse National Military Park, GUCO1492 and GUCO1625, p. 11 (bottom); Photos.com, p. 10; Public Domain Image, p. 20; Shutterstock.com, p. 11 (top); Steven Wynn / Photos.com, p. 18.

Cover Illustration: The Granger Collection, NYC (Mrs. Philip Schuyler, wife of the Continental Army general, fires her cornfields near Saratoga, New York, at the approach of British forces in 1777).

CONTENTS

⎯⎯⎯ ★ ⎯⎯⎯

LOOK FOR THIS SYMBOL **PRIMARY SOURCE** TO FIND THE PRIMARY SOURCES THROUGHOUT THIS BOOK.

During the American Revolution, women and children supported the war effort in many ways. In this illustration, women and children work at various activities in a colonial kitchen.

CHAPTER 1

★

THE ROLES OF WOMEN AND CHILDREN

"Washed . . . Ironed . . . Scoured rooms . . . Pulled radishes . . . Killed the pig . . . Made bread . . . Made 5 shirts for the doctor . . . did other things."[1] This entry from the diary of Mary Holyoke provides a glimpse at women's work around the time of the American Revolution. Life was hard.

Women worked hard, but they had few rights. For the most part, they could not vote. Women rarely owned homes or businesses. Husbands owned all the property. When they died, the family's land passed on to their sons.

Few married women held jobs outside the home. Their job was to run the house, take care of the children, and help their

Fun and Games

Most children had little time to play. Many of their games were simple ones that did not need much equipment. Children played hopscotch, leapfrog, and hide and seek. Some flew kites, played marbles, and jumped rope. Popular toys included tops and dolls.[2]

husbands in any way they needed. Women rarely had any time to relax. Each task had to be done by hand. There was no electric power or running water.

The proper role for a woman, people of the time thought, was to be a wife and mother. Women who did not marry were called spinsters. People looked down on them.

Married women spent much of their lives having and raising children. Some women had a baby every couple of years over a period of twenty years or more. Having children was dangerous.

Most babies were born at home. If there were any problems, both mother and child were at risk. Often, women died in childbirth. Many children died young, too.[3]

Even if they survived, children lived a hard life. After infancy, they were treated as little adults. Even young children did chores. They fetched water and cleaned the house. They fed the farm animals. Most children had little time for play.

Many communities worked to provide schools. But few children had a chance to attend. They had to work around the house or farm. Those who did attend often found that the school lacked supplies, such as books and writing tools.

At the age of fourteen or so, many boys became apprentices. This meant that they were training to learn trades. Three important trades were blacksmith, shoemaker, and cooper. Blacksmiths made items of metal. Coopers made barrels and other wooden containers. As apprentices, boys often learned to read, write, and do math. These skills were part of the business.[4]

Most girls were taught at home. Many parents thought it was more important for girls to spend time doing household chores than to spend time in school.[5] In many homes, mothers taught their daughters to read and write. Some girls learned a lot this way. Others learned little. It all depended on how much their mothers knew and how much time they had to spend teaching.

Most women from wealthy homes did receive an education. Some went to school. Others had private teachers. Some women, such as Abigail Adams, wanted more women to get an education. Abigail often talked to her husband, colonial leader John Adams, about women's rights. These included the right to education and the right to vote.

During the time leading up to the war, women's roles began to expand. Many women became active in the protests against English taxes. In 1767, the British passed a law called the Townshend Act. This act taxed goods imported, or brought over, from England. In protest, many colonists boycotted. They did not buy British goods.

Abigail Adams, shown here in this portrait made in 1800, often spoke to her husband about women's rights. She wanted women to have the right to vote and to get an education.

Women in Business

Some women did run businesses, either on their own or on behalf of their families. Before the American Revolution, when she was still a teenager, Eliza Lucas Pinckney ran three plantations. Over the years, she became wealthy.

Benjamin Franklin traveled often. While he was gone, his wife, Deborah, ran his printing business. She also helped run the postal service after Franklin was made postmaster for the colonies.

Deborah Franklin (seated) helped run her husband's businesses while Benjamin (standing) traveled as an ambassador for the United States during the American Revolution.

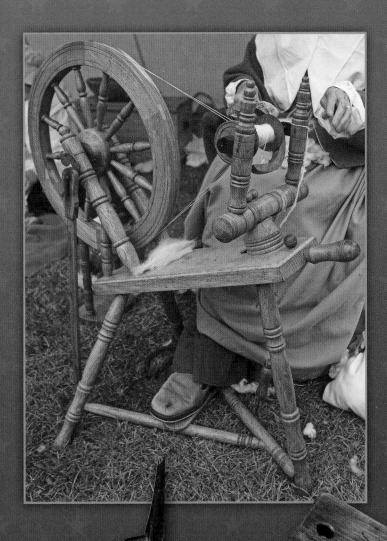

PRIMARY
SOURCE

To protest Britain's taxes on imported cloth, many women gathered for "spinning bees." The top photo shows a reconstructed spinning wheel. The artifacts shown are colonial-era tools used for spinning. The niddy noddy (left) was used for measuring wool yarn for weaving. The flax comb (right) was used to make the fibers of material clean and straight before spinning.

Some women gathered for "spinning bees." There, they wove cloth by hand. This meant that they did not have to buy the cloth from England. By doing so, they were helping "the public good," wrote one newspaper.[6] Later, women helped support the boycott of English tea. They did the shopping, and they refused to buy tea from England.

Women lacked legal rights, but many wives held the real power in their homes. In most cases, their husbands spent their days working. They spent evenings with other men talking about relations with England. In the meantime, their wives controlled the household. They ran the homes and raised the children. They made the day-to-day decisions. The men handled global affairs. "The women," one writer noted, "handled pretty much everything else."[7]

CHAPTER 2

HOLDING DOWN THE HOME FRONT

"*Here I sit on Buttermilk Hill*

Who can blame me, cry my fill?

And every tear would turn a mill,

Since Johnny has gone for a soldier."[1]

This song, popular during the war, sums up how many families felt. Fighting raged from 1775 to 1781. Many men enlisted in the army. Some served only a few months. Others served through the entire war.

With husbands away fighting the war, women's burdens grew. They continued to run the homes. They cooked, cleaned, and

This photo shows a reconstructed colonial-era kitchen. On the home front during the American Revolution, women had to take on many responsibilities. In addition to cooking, cleaning, and raising children, women needed to run farms and businesses.

raised the children. Often they had to run their husbands' farms or businesses, too. There was always work to do.

Over time, women began to feel some ownership. Early in the war, Mary Bartlett wrote to her husband about the status of "your farming business." After a couple of years, she began to refer to it as "our farming business."[2]

People who lived in areas where fighting took place faced even greater problems. Armies from both sides often took over private homes. They camped on the land. Sometimes they even made families take officers into their homes. Soldiers raided people's livestock and gardens. In the South, the British sometimes took slaves with them when they left an area.[3]

Eliza Wilkinson reported that the British took all her extra clothes. They even took the buckles from the shoes she was wearing.[4] When a British officer took over the home of Elizabeth Drinker of Philadelphia, she complained that he moved in with "3 horses, 2 cows, 2 sheep, and 2 turkeys." He even brought his servants.[5]

Poet Ann Eliza Bleecker suffered even more. She left her home in northern New York as British general John Burgoyne's army approached. She feared the British would harm her and her infant, Abella. She took her daughter and fled to the woods. The baby died of cold and hunger.[6]

Women did more than just support the war effort through their work at home. Many helped in other important ways. To help clothe the soldiers, some states set quotas. Cities had to provide a certain amount of clothing for the Continental Army.

Women's Rights

In 1776, John Adams went off to Philadelphia. There, he helped prepare the Declaration of Independence. His wife, Abigail, urged him to "remember the ladies."[7] She hoped that ladies would soon have many of the same rights men did. Throughout her life, Abigail kept speaking out for women's rights. Change was a long time coming, however.

In 1776, women in Hartford, Connecticut, had to make 1,000 coats and vests and 1,600 shirts.[8]

In 1780, Esther De Berdt Reed of Philadelphia wanted to raise money for the patriot cause. She gathered a group of thirty-six women. They went door-to-door collecting money. Within a month, they had gathered thousands of dollars.

The women wanted General George Washington to give the money to his soldiers. Washington had other ideas. He wanted the money used to make shirts for the soldiers. He even asked the ladies to make these shirts themselves in order to save money. By December 1780, the ladies had made 2,000 shirts. They told the general, "We wish them to be worn with as much pleasure as they were made."[9]

Children, too, took on added responsibility because of the war. If their fathers were away fighting, they did tasks, such as plowing and harvesting crops. They also helped even more with the household chores. This gave the women more time to run the family's farm or business. Many children also had to cope with the loss of a loved one killed or captured in battle.

In some cases, children saw the harsh and violent realities of war up close. On September 11, 1777, eight-year-old Sarah Frazer was sent home from her school in Thornbury, Pennsylvania.

This illustration shows women and children helping arm the Minutemen before they leave for Lexington after receiving the first battle alarm.

Legendary Flag Maker

Betsy Ross sat sewing in her shop one spring day in 1776. As the legend goes, three men entered. One of them was General George Washington. The men told her they wanted her to make a flag. They showed her the basic design for a flag with stripes and six-pointed stars. The legend says she suggested that the stars have five points instead. She showed them how such stars could easily be made. She went on to make that first flag and many others during the war.[10]

Did Betsy Ross really sew that first flag? Some experts think she did. Others disagree. We do know that Betsy Ross made many early flags in her home on Arch Street in Philadelphia. She ran her flag-making business for more than fifty years.

Betsy Ross

There is no proof that Betsy Ross made the first American flag, but she did make many early flags from her home in Philadelphia. This replica Betsy Ross flag flies outside city hall in San Francisco, California.

British troops were nearby. Soon, the Battle of Brandywine began along a creek west of Philadelphia. Her mother rushed off toward the battle to check on Sarah's father. He was a colonel in the Continental Army. Colonel Persifor Frazer survived the battle unharmed. Soon after, however, the British captured him. He spent the winter in a British prison. Like many other families, the Frazers had to cope on their own.[11]

CHAPTER 3

☆

FOLLOWING THE ARMY

Many women and children traveled with one of the armies during the war. These people were called "camp followers." Some experts estimate that as many as 20,000 women traveled with the Continental Army over the course of the war.[1] Some women followed the army because they had no homes. Others were unable to maintain the homes they had while their husbands were away fighting. If they stayed on their farms or in their homes, they faced loneliness or even starvation.

Often camp followers were refugees who fled as the enemy army approached. They feared being harmed by enemy troops.

Nursing the Wounded

During the war, more soldiers died from illness than in battle. Diseases, such as smallpox, killed many troops. Many other illnesses resulted from poor sanitation in camps, as human waste was often not disposed of properly.

Some women served as nurses in the army. Often nurses were more like servants. They scrubbed floors, cooked meals, and washed dishes. In 1777, nurses earned eight dollars per month. General Washington wanted to hire more nurses and pay them better. Having more female nurses would free up male nurses to serve in battle. His idea was not acted upon.[2]

About three-fourths of Boston's civilians fled the city—which was controlled by the British army—soon after the war broke out in 1775.[3] Likewise, many left Philadelphia when the British took over the city in 1777. For days, wagons left town "filled with household goods and people in flight."[4] Some of them ended up as camp followers of Washington's army.

The British army also had camp followers. This engraving shows Hessian mercenaries, soldiers hired by the British, on a march with their camp followers during the American Revolution.

General Washington realized the value of camp followers. But he also thought they slowed the army down. In 1777, he urged his officers to "get rid of all such as are not absolutely necessary."[5] He also said that women were to travel at the rear of the army with the baggage. He did not want them riding in the supply wagons.

The British army had camp followers, too. In fact, by 1781, the British had one woman for every 4.5 soldiers.[6] This was more than the Continental Army had.

Camp followers provided needed services for the army. Just washing the soldiers' clothes was a huge job. Women earned money for their work. They did not earn much, though. In 1780, at one American camp, women earned two shillings per shirt.[7] That was equal to just a few cents.

Women camp followers also helped the army in other ways. Some served as nurses. Others cooked. "It would not do for men to fight and starve, too," wrote Sarah Osborn, a cook for George Washington's army.[8]

Although Martha Washington did not like being near the battles, she often traveled with the Continental Army to support her husband and his troops. This 1798 engraving shows George Washington, Martha, her two grandchildren, and William Lee, an African-American slave who was George Washington's personal servant.

Martha Washington

The most famous spouse to stay with the Continental Army was Martha Washington. She did not travel with the army year round, as some women did. However, each winter she left the comfort of her home at Mount Vernon, Virginia, to be with her husband and his troops. She helped cheer up the soldiers during the long winter at Valley Forge. She visited sick soldiers in their huts. She also took charge of making the meals at George Washington's headquarters.[9]

Martha did not enjoy camp life. She found the sounds of war frightening. "I confess I shudder every time I hear the sound of a gun," she later recalled of joining her husband with the army for the first time.[10] Still, she stayed. Her presence made life easier for George.

Camp followers had a hard life. Other people looked down on them. One woman described British camp followers as poor, dirty, and smelly. The group included "some very young infants who were born on the road, the women [in] bare feet, clothed in dirty rags."[11]

Children suffered in this life. They had no real home. They had to travel wherever the army traveled. They could not always get food rations or fresh water. In winter, shelter could be hard to find.

Still, many families lived this way during the war. They had no other choice.

CHAPTER 4

AT THE BATTLEFRONT

High above the Hudson River north of New York City, the defenders of Fort Washington prepared for battle. They were completely surrounded. The rest of the Continental Army had been driven away.

Among those inside the fort on November 16, 1776, were John Corbin and his wife, Margaret. John fired a cannon during the early part of the battle. Margaret helped him load the weapon. Then he fell dead, struck by British cannon fire.

Margaret stepped into John's place. She began to load and fire the cannon herself. Then she, too, was wounded by British cannon fire. She was captured but later released by the redcoats.

Her wound caused her to lose the use of her left arm. She received a pension from the army because of her injury.[1] (A pension is a sum of money paid regularly to someone for past service.)

Private Robert Shurtleff drilled, marched, and fought. In one skirmish, he was slashed by a saber. In another, he was shot in the thigh. He served bravely for about eighteen months. Then Robert came down with a bad fever. He was taken to a hospital. There, the doctor discovered that Robert had a secret. "Robert" was really a woman named Deborah Sampson.

The doctor sent Sampson to General Washington, who gave her a discharge. Years later, he invited her to come to Congress. Congress gave her a pension and some land.[2] After the war, Sampson traveled around giving lectures. At the end of her speech, she marched across the stage in her old army uniform.[3]

Several other women also fought disguised as men. Sally St. Clair kept her secret throughout the war until she died in battle. A few women whose secret was exposed were treated poorly. Many men thought women should stay at home, not fight in battle.

Molly Pitcher

The legend of Molly Pitcher sprang from the Battle of Monmouth in June 1778. General Washington's troops fought the British on a steaming hot day. According to legend, Mary (Molly) Hays carried water to the troops in a pitcher throughout the battle.

Molly's husband fired a cannon. In between carrying water to thirsty men and carrying water to cool down the cannons, she helped pass the cartridges. One soldier later wrote that an enemy cannonball passed right through her legs, tearing away part of her dress. She kept working. Other versions of the legend have her taking over the cannon after her husband is killed by enemy fire.

Many historians say that "Molly Pitcher" did not really exist. The name referred to "the many women who carried water to cool down the cannons so that soldiers could reload and fire them again."[4]

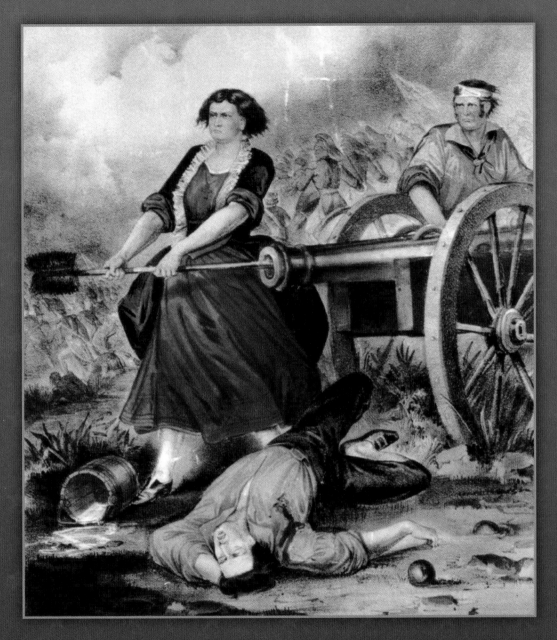

The legend of Molly Pitcher, depicted in this dramatic illustration, said she carried water to soldiers during the Battle of Monmouth and took over the cannon after her husband was shot down. Historians believe that Molly Pitcher was not a real person, but a symbol for the many brave women who aided American soldiers in battle.

Deborah Sampson

Only a few women fought in the war. However, many young boys did. Technically, boys under the age of sixteen were not allowed to serve in the army. In reality, many signed up. Some did so to fight for their country's freedom. Others sought adventure. Still others wanted the modest enlistment bonus—twenty dollars, a new suit of clothes, and one hundred acres of land if they enlisted for the entire war.[5]

Peer pressure convinced some young boys to enlist. Fifteen-year-old Joseph Plumb Martin thought of his friends who had joined the army. He heard stories of battle told by other soldiers. All this, as he put it, began "to warm my courage."[6] Martin enlisted in 1776. He planned to spend six months in the army. Instead, he ended up serving throughout the rest of the war.

A NEW

TOUCH ON THE TIMES.

Well adapted to the distressing situation of every Sea-port Town.

By a DAUGHTER OF LIBERTY, living in MARBLEHEAD.

OUR best beloved they are gone,
We cannot tell they'll e'er return,
For they are gone the ocean wide,
Which for us now they must provide.
  For they go on the roaring seas,
For which we can't get any ease,
For they are gone to work for us,
And that it is to fill our purse.
  And to fill our houses too,
What more could we then have them do?
They now do more then we deserve,
Wan't it for them we now should starve,
Starve then we should and perish too,
And without them what could we do?
  We must do as well as we can,
What could women do without man,
They could not do by night or day,
Go round the world and that they'll say.
  They could not do by day or night,
I think that man's a woman's delight,
It's hard and cruel times to live,
Takes thirty dollars to buy a sieve.
  To buy sieves and other things too,
To go thro' the world how can we do,
For times they sure grow worse and worse,
I'm sure it sinks our scanty purse.
  Had we a purse to reach the sky,
It would be all just vanity,
If we had shit and ten times more,
'Twould be like sand upon the shore.
  For money is not worth a pin,
Had we but salt we've any thing,
For salt is all the Farmer's cry,
If we've no salt we sure must die.
  We can't get fire nor yet food,
Takes 20 weight of sugar for two foot of wood,
We cannot get bread nor yet meat,
We see the world is nought but cheat.
  We cannot now get meat nor bread
By means of which we shake
All we can get it is but rice,
And that is of a wretched price.

And as we go up and down,
We see the doings of this town,
Some say they an't victuals nor drink,
Others say they are ready to sink.
  Our lives they all are tired here,
We see all things so cruel dear,
Nothing now-a-days to be got,
To put in kettle nor in pot.
  These times will learn us to be wise,
We now do eat what we despis'd:
I now have something more to say,
We must go up and down the Bay.
  To get a fish a-days to fry,
We can't get fat were we to die,
Were we to try all thro' the town,
The world is now turn'd up-side down.
  But there's a gracious God above,
That deals with us in tender love,
If we be kind and just and true,
He'll set and turn the world anew.
  If we'll repent of all our crimes,
He'll set us new new heavenly times,
Times that will make us all to ring,
If we forsake our heinous sins.
  For sin is all the cause of this,
We must not take it then amiss,
Wan't it for our polluted tongues
This cruel war would ne'er begun.
  We should hear no fife nor drum,
Nor training bands would never come,
Should we go on our sinful course,
Times will grow on us worse and worse.
  Then, gracious God now cause to cease,
This bloody war and give us peace!
And down our streets send plenty then,
With hearts as one we'll say Amen!
  If we expect to be forgiv'n,
Let's tread the road that leads to Heav'n
In these times we can't rub along.
I now have ended this my song.
  MOLLY GUTRIDGE compositie
  Be sure it is no imposition.

This 1779 broadside features a poem describing the hardships of the American Revolution, written by a Daughter of Liberty from Marblehead, Massachusetts. A woodcut of a female Continental soldier appears in the upper right hand corner.

Front-Row Seat to History

Many boys and young men served in the army during the American Revolution. Few witnessed as many key events as John Greenwood. He joined the army at the age of fifteen. He served during the siege of Boston in 1775 and 1776. Then he took part in the American invasion of Canada. He returned to join Washington's troops in the stirring triumph at Trenton.

Later in the war, Greenwood served at sea. He helped capture several British ships.

After the war, he opened a dental practice in New York City. In the 1790s, he made false teeth for President Washington.[7]

Teenager Ebenezer Fox was serving as an apprentice barber when the shop owner was drafted. The owner convinced Fox to go in his place. Boys such as Martin and Fox were by no means the youngest fighters. David Hamilton Morris joined the army at age eleven.[8]

CHAPTER 5

★

SPIES AND MESSENGERS

The rider sped through the dark April night. At each door, the rider warned that British troops were coming. The militia needed to turn out. It sounds like the famous story of Paul Revere, but it is not. It is the story of Sybil Ludington. The sixteen-year-old girl traveled the roads of Putnam County, New York, in April 1777. She alerted the militia that British troops were moving toward Danbury, Connecticut. They planned to destroy the arms depot there. The British did destroy the arms, but the militia then helped drive the troops away.[1]

Other women, too, did daring deeds during the war. In Georgia, a slave known as Mammy Kate rode fifty miles to visit her master. He had been captured by loyalists and placed in jail. He feared being killed. Mammy Kate smuggled him out of jail in a laundry basket.[2]

In South Carolina, a young girl named Emily Geiger was carrying a written message from General Nathanael Greene to another American general. When she was captured by the British, Emily tore the paper into small pieces. Then she ate them before the British could find anything. After they released her, she rode on and told the general the message.[3]

Sixteen-year-old Sybil Ludington also went on a famous ride to warn the colonial militia that British troops were coming to Putnam County, New York, in April 1777. Throughout the war, many children and women served as spies and messengers.

Men, women, and children alike served as spies. Nathan Hale became the war's best-known spy, even though he was captured and killed. Just before he was hanged, he is said to have spoken the famous words, "I only regret that I have but one life to lose for my country."[4]

A Big Bang

Some women spied and carried messages for the army. Others stored guns and gunpowder. In South Carolina, Martha Bratton had supplies and ammunition hidden in her home. The British found out. They sent loyalists to seize the supplies.

Bratton laid a trail of gunpowder from the supplies to a spot outside her home. When the loyalists arrived, she lit the gunpowder. Moments later, a huge explosion destroyed Bratton's home. She was willing to pay that price to keep the supplies out of British hands.[5]

Mammy Kate, a Georgia slave, helped smuggle her master out of jail in a laundry basket after loyalists had captured him.

Women and children made good spies. They could quietly gather and deliver information. Few people suspected them. They came up with clever ways to pass on what they had learned. One woman sent messages by the way she hung her laundry. A woman named Lydia Darragh sent coded messages hidden in her son's coat buttons.[6]

The British had spies, too. One of the best was Ann Bates. She was fearless. One time, she managed to get right inside Washington's headquarters. There she was able to find out about his army's troop strength, along with the number of cannons they had.[7]

that a Woman whom Craig
has trusted often — came to town
last night — she is well acquainted
with many of the R. A — a particular
known to Chalmers — one who
C. B. transacted a great deal of
business with — it is proposed to
send her out, under the Idea
of selling little Matters in the
R. C. she will converse with
Chambers; a will return whenever
she may have learnt any thing
that shall be deserved to be known

234: 27

Ann Bates worked as a spy for General Henry Clinton and the British army. Posing as a peddler under the fake name Mrs. Barnes, Bates sold her goods to Americans while secretly reporting information to the British. Major Drummond, the leader of Clinton's spy network, is thought to have written this letter about Bates.

The Overheard Plans

America hung on by a thread at the end of 1777. The British held Philadelphia, America's capital. They took over many private homes, including the home of Lydia Darragh. Washington's army, stationed a few miles outside of town, was weak. One blow might finish the Americans. In early December, the British planned a surprise attack.

Darragh listened outside the room where the British were meeting. She overheard their plan. The next day, she sneaked out of town. She made sure the news reached Washington. When the British attacked, they found the American troops ready. The British quickly fell back.[8]

General Washington thought that spies were very important. He formed a large spy network. His spies helped him throughout the war. And many of his best spies were women and children.

They joined other brave women and children who wanted freedom for their country. These patriots helped the United States win its independence.

TIMELINE

Prewar

In 1767, the British pass the Townshend Act, which places taxes on many goods imported from England. In protest, colonists boycott British goods. In some areas, women gather to make goods to replace the imported items that are no longer available.

In 1773, colonists rebel against taxes on tea. Again, women have an important role in the protests.

1775

War begins in April with battles at Lexington and Concord in Massachusetts. Many women watch their husbands march off to war. They are left to tend the family farms and businesses in addition to running the household.

Many young boys, including John Greenwood, enlist in the Continental Army.

1776

According to legend, Betsy Ross receives a visit from General Washington, who asks her to make a flag for the Continental Army.

Abigail Adams urges her husband, John, to "remember the ladies" when he and other leaders meet to frame the Declaration of Independence.

In November, Margaret Corbin is injured while fighting at the battle of Fort Washington in New York. She later receives an army pension.

1777

The British defeat American troops at the Battle of Brandywine on September 11. They soon capture Philadelphia.

The British turn back an American assault at Germantown on October 4.

On October 17, a British army surrenders in Saratoga, New York.

Lydia Darragh of Philadelphia smuggles out details of a planned British surprise attack on the American troops at Whitemarsh. Because of her spy work, the Americans are ready. The British attack fails.

1778

France signs a treaty of alliance with the United States and declares war on England.

The legend of Molly Pitcher begins after the Battle of Monmouth in June. Mary (Molly) Hays is said to have carried water to the troops throughout the battle and to have fired an American cannon after its regular crew was injured or killed.

1779–1780

Disguised as a man, Sally St. Clair dies in fighting at the Battle of Savannah in 1779. She had kept her secret throughout the war.

In 1780, Esther De Berdt Reed, wife of the governor of Pennsylvania, and other women raise thousands of dollars for the Continental Army.

1781–1783

Camp follower Sarah Osborn, a cook for General Washington's army, witnesses the victory at Yorktown in October 1781.

In 1783, the Treaty of Paris is signed, officially ending the war. The British recognize American independence.

Postwar

Deborah Sampson, who had fought for about eighteen months during the war disguised as a man, gives lectures around the country describing her experiences.

CHAPTER NOTES

CHAPTER 1: THE ROLES OF WOMEN AND CHILDREN

1. Carol Berkin, *Revolutionary Mothers: Women in the Struggle for America's Independence* (New York: Knopf, 2005), p. 8.
2. Dale Taylor, *The Writer's Guide to Everyday Life in Colonial America From 1607–1783* (Cincinnati: Writer's Digest Books, 1997), p. 137.
3. Cokie Roberts, *Founding Mothers: The Women Who Raised Our Nation* (New York: HarperCollins, 2004), p. 13.
4. Taylor, pp. 236–237.
5. Alice Morse Earle, *Child Life in Colonial Days* (Stockbridge, Mass.: Berkshire House Publishers, 1993), p. 90.
6. Ray Raphael, *A People's History of the American Revolution: How Common People Shaped the Fight for Independence* (New York: The New Press, 2001), p. 108.
7. Roberts, p. 14.

CHAPTER 2: HOLDING DOWN THE HOME FRONT

1. Carol Berkin, *Revolutionary Mothers: Women in the Struggle for America's Independence* (New York: Knopf, 2005), p. 31.
2. Ray Raphael, *A People's History of the American Revolution: How Common People Shaped the Fight for Independence* (New York: The New Press, 2001), p. 114.
3. Berkin, p. 34.
4. Sally Smith Booth, *The Women of '76* (New York: Hastings House, 1973), p. 259.
5. Berkin, p. 35.
6. Ibid., p. 37.
7. Cokie Roberts, *Founding Mothers: The Women Who Raised Our Nation* (New York: HarperCollins, 2004), p. xvi.
8. Raphael, p. 118.

9. Ibid., p. 116.

10. John Balderston Harker, *Betsy Ross's Five Pointed Star* (Melbourne Beach, Fla.: Canmore Press, 2004), pp. 37–38.

11. Wayne Bodle, *The Valley Forge Winter: Civilians and Soldiers in War* (University Park, Pa.: The Pennsylvania State University Press, 2002), pp. 78–79.

CHAPTER 3: FOLLOWING THE ARMY

1. Carol Berkin, *Revolutionary Mothers: Women in the Struggle for America's Independence* (New York: Knopf, 2005), p. 52.

2. Oscar Reiss, *Medicine and the American Revolution* (Jefferson, N.C.: McFarland & Company, Inc., 1998), p. 45.

3. Ray Raphael, *A People's History of the American Revolution: How Common People Shaped the Fight for Independence* (New York: The New Press, 2001), p. 135.

4. Wayne Bodle, *The Valley Forge Winter: Civilians and Soldiers in War* (University Park, Pa.: The Pennsylvania State University Press, 2002), p. 17.

5. Sally Smith Booth, *The Women of '76* (New York: Hastings House, 1973), p. 183.

6. Raphael, p. 124.

7. Berkin, p. 57.

8. Raphael, p. 120.

9. Thomas Fleming, *Washington's Secret War: The Hidden History of Valley Forge* (New York: HarperCollins, 2005), p. 185.

10. Cokie Roberts, *Founding Mothers: The Women Who Raised Our Nation* (New York: HarperCollins, 2004), p. 87.

11. Raphael, p. 124.

CHAPTER 4: **AT THE BATTLEFRONT**

1. Carol Berkin, *Revolutionary Mothers: Women in the Struggle for America's Independence* (New York: Knopf, 2005), pp. 138–139.
2. Cokie Roberts, *Founding Mothers: The Women Who Raised Our Nation* (New York: HarperCollins, 2004), p. 82.
3. Sally Smith Booth, *The Women of '76* (New York: Hastings House, 1973), p. 268.
4. Berkin, p. xi.
5. Ray Raphael, *A People's History of the American Revolution: How Common People Shaped the Fight for Independence* (New York: The New Press, 2001), p. 63.
6. Jim Murphy, *A Young Patriot: The American Revolution as Experienced By One Boy* (New York: Clarion, 1996), pp. 14–15.
7. John Greenwood, *A Young Patriot in the American Revolution* (n.p.: Westvaco, 1981), various pages.
8. Raphael, p. 62.

CHAPTER 5: **SPIES AND MESSENGERS**

1. Carol Berkin, *Revolutionary Mothers: Women in the Struggle for America's Independence* (New York: Knopf, 2005), p. 139.
2. Ibid., p. 142.
3. Ibid., p. 145.
4. Thomas Fleming, *Liberty! The American Revolution* (New York: Viking, 1997), p. 206.
5. Berkin, pp. 143–144.
6. Cokie Roberts, *Founding Mothers: The Women Who Raised Our Nation* (New York: HarperCollins, 2004), p. 80.
7. Berkin, p. 141.
8. Sally Smith Booth, *The Women of '76* (New York: Hastings House, 1973), pp. 154–155.

GLOSSARY

apprentice—A person who works for another to learn a trade.

boycott—To refuse to use certain goods or services, often as a form of protest.

camp follower—A woman or child who traveled with the army, often providing services such as cooking and washing clothes.

cartridge—A paper tube containing a measured amount of gunpowder for use in firing a round from a cannon or firearm.

cooper—A person who makes or repairs casks or barrels.

depot—A place where arms or supplies are stored.

discharge—To release a soldier from military service.

imported—Brought in from another source, usually another country.

loyalist—An American who supported the British during the Revolutionary War.

militia—Citizens who enroll for military service. They drill from time to time but serve full time only in emergencies.

pension—A fixed amount paid at regular times for past service.

plantation—A large farm or estate on which crops such as cotton or tobacco are grown.

primary source—A document, text, or physical object that was written or created during the time under discussion.

quota—A goal or assignment of goods to be produced.

rations—An allowance of food for civilians or soldiers.

saber—A heavy, one-edged sword.

skirmish—A fight between small units of armies, as opposed to a full battle.

spinster—An unmarried woman, usually beyond the age when most women are married.

FURTHER READING

Books

Anderson, Dale. *Daily Life During the American Revolution.* Milwaukee, Wis.: World Almanac Library, 2006.

Fleming, Thomas. *Everybody's Revolution: A New Look at the People Who Won America's Freedom.* New York: Scholastic Nonfiction, 2006.

Taschek, Karen. *Daughters of Liberty: The American Revolution and the Early Republic, 1775–1827.* New York: Chelsea House Publishers, 2011.

Walsh, Francis. *Daring Women of the American Revolution.* New York: PowerKids Press, 2009.

Internet Addresses

PBS: The Men and Women of Liberty!
<http://www.pbs.org/ktca/liberty/liberty_menwomen.html>

The American Revolution: An Everyday Life Perspective
<http://maass.nyu.edu/resources/r1/index.html>

INDEX